Comestibles

Comestibles

Kathleen Burnham

RESOURCE *Publications* · Eugene, Oregon

COMESTIBLES

Resource Publications
An Imprint of Wipf and Stock Publishers
199 W. 8th Ave., Suite 3
Eugene, OR 97401

www.wipfandstock.com

PAPERBACK ISBN: 978-1-7252-9597-1
HARDCOVER ISBN: 978-1-7252-9596-4
EBOOK ISBN: 978-1-7252-9598-8

03/10/21

"Red Wings Collapsing," copyright Emily Pettit.

Lolita, copyright Vladimir Nabokov.

To my son, Bob. I love you with all my heart.
You are my heart and my reason and my warrant.

Contents

CONTENTS

Preface

In composing this collection, I didn't know what I was really writing about, what I was forming as a whole. I went to write about anything other than what I *did* end up writing, and that was about the loss of my loved ones and my affair culminating in pregnancy, in an angry, hungry voice. I realized three things about my work in these poems—I am obsessed with coffee, tea, and its accoutrements; I tend to equate life's mile-markers and sharing love with sharing really good food; poetry is very deeply entwined with consumption and feeling nurtured/giving succor to the psyche through sound, vision, and mouthfeel. We consume anything and everything because we need to feel fed, full. All the most recognized art taps into this primal first need. Consumptive need forms our language and expression from birth to adulthood; becoming a mother while studying to evolve as a poet has taught me that. It doesn't help that I was once an apprentice chef, prior to my jumping on the BA in English wagon. I'm not the only one who has drawn these conclusions—poet, chef, or otherwise—if it's any consolation.

Donald Hall talked about mouthfeel and the consumptive need to latch on to the primal nurture of language and sound in his essay "Goatfoot, Milktongue, and Twinbird: the Psychic Origins of Poetry." He supplied the metaphor of a child experiencing the "forepleasure" of infancy and having all of its needs met, enjoying the simplest forms of the sensual in cooing, suckling, and being almost purely physical in its interactions. Even non-poets recognize the connection between language, nurturing, and consumption, hearkening back to the desire for feeling a sense of place and authenticity of being.

I find this truth present in every art form, the way that the golden rule is present in so many religions and faiths. Our first music is the rhythmic pulse of blood whirring in the mother, what feeds us through the umbilical cord. Artists, poets, composers, they are the shamans of complex society in its spiritually divested state, interpreting wisdom, the ineffable—bringing sense and reason into dialogue. Of course, all of the poems collected here face my family, my path to becoming a mother, and doing it the hard way; I realize that many of my poems are rendered through the lens of the visceral, of consumption, being consumed, and swallowing down words and emotions only to bring them back up to chew over. If there isn't a pie, there is coffee, and if not coffee there is something baking in the oven nearby, as near as death or sex or birthing a child. My first MFA mentor, Nickole Brown, told me that the main themes that are at the bottom of every work of literature or verse are Love, Death, and Sex. We should add Birth and Food to that list. I think my work here does that.

Sin Eater

I will burn in Hell
when I die, lover.

I'm certain
because I often
wake up—in terror
sweat—from a
peaceful, quiet,
black-out slumber,
afraid of my coming
flat line. My body
knows something
my subconscious
is obfuscating,
choking on.

A confessionary
prayer my conscience
has swallowed in
contrition like
bread, wine, salt.

There's also that bit
about lying to your
wife about sleeping
with you every week,
when I'm not making
her breakfast or
driving her daughter
to school. I choke
on that too.

Amen.

Shadowbox Menagerie

She reclines in her favorite chair while I
perch on the edge of the sofa, poised for
escape. Her hands toy with remote control
buttons. Mine tinker with tools: tape, tissue,
safety scissors, a dust rag, and patience. I am
wrapping her baubles in bubble paper,
delicately, meticulously—my lover's wife.

I count them—1, 2, 3 . . . 43 . . . 83 . . . —a seashell,
a doll-sized flower pot, an eraser in the shape of
a ladybug, a porcelain rabbit, a piece of metallic
confetti. Each item has a slot in the box containing
the whole menagerie, and I wonder if she really
believes in Jesus or in the pewter pocket reminder
stamped with a cross and the Lord's Prayer. I swab
and polish each relic before cocooning it in the tissue,
feeling their weight and counting them like rosary beads.
Am I doing penance? Have I trespassed against her,
or has she invited me in like the vampire I am?

A funny commercial plays on the television screen.
She giggles, winks, asks me how my dog is doing.
I wonder what God is doing. I smile, trim tissue, pull
tape tabs, and take controlled breaths. My phone buzzes—
my lover asks me, "How is it going?" I reply, "This is
taking forever!" What I want to do is dig my fingers
into my own flesh, scream until my throat bleeds, leave
my body in a bloody lump on the floor in front of their sofa.
Text messages cannot convey those sentiments effectually.

At around 9:30PM, I finish wrapping and packing
knick-knacks into cardboard boxes. She says,
"Thank you. You are our angel." I think:
I *make love to him, and you* don't.

I *wrap* your *thingamabob collection, and* he *doesn't.*
I *listen to your woes and secrets and talk about*
menstrual cycles and parenting concerns. Our three
separate roles are mixed up beyond un-puzzling—
I'm fucking your husband tomorrow night, and I
have no idea who is fucking you, and I'm actually
concerned about how happy you are.

He texts me, "You don't have to help us like this."
I respond, "And miss this quality psycho time?"
He says I make him smile.
Then she hugs me.

Definition of Insanity

This time will be different.

> Your eyes—huge, crystalline, jeweled
> like candied fruit, dripping and slick.
> I gently press them shut, sip away
> the tears that seep, well up from
> those weathered window sills.

This time *will* be different.

> Coax me through the labyrinth
> constructed to keep most tourists out,
> seeing the *crack* in you that is *in everything*
> *God has made, where the light enters.* How
> you turned inward—a cluster of healthy cells
> attacked, evolving abnormally, metamorphosing.

This time *it* will be *different.*

> Unfolding, unfurling. Teeth no longer jail bars.
> Absorbing the poison in your skin through my
> own body, a church where you go to pray—
> violent, unabashed, selfish, parishioner.
> Eating your darkness.

This time was a diagnosis.

> An austere convent of a marriage, with a Mother
> Superior expecting devotion, abstinence, celibacy.
> Sleeping in different rooms, never touch, never speak.
> Protecting you from yourself was never an option, and
> this time was no different—letting me into your heart only
> for me to find it filled with little boxes, compartmentalized—
> offering only one little box to work on, labeled with my own name.

** "crack...everything...where the light enters" quoted from Ralph Waldo Emerson and Rumi: "There is a crack in everything God has made" and "The wound is where the light enters you."

How to Escape Losing

I start with the hair—buzz it off
to nothing but duck fluff. Then
the shoes—of the twenty-something
pairs I own, cut it down to three.
Clear the closet of all the dresses
for special occasions. Put away
the jewelry I never wear and throw
out the makeup I never don due to
never feeling pretty enough to pull it
off. Donate all of Grandma's wartime
porcelain trinkets made in occupied
Japan—they collect the dust of her
absence. Toss my coin collection into
any lake, fountain, or stream, where
they might buy wishes when they can't
buy anything else. Don't wish on them.
Push full the extra-flex garbage bags
with decades-old greeting cards and
love letters, work-logo sweatshirts,
coffee mugs, chef coats, name tags,
and souvenirs. Defile the shrine of
my house that has become a pyramid
tomb in the guise of a hope chest. It
won't follow me into the dark, where
I am following it. Give it all away
before I lose it, and avoid losing
altogether. My last bastion is the
body. How I love it and how it fades.

Clausius and Thomson's Second Law of Thermodynamics

—In response to Matthew Olzmann's "Sir Isaac Newton's First Law of Motion"

As energy is transferred or transformed, more and more of it is
wasted. There is a natural tendency of any isolated system to
degenerate into a more disordered state. Randomness and chaos
increase. Kate Burnham is an isolated system, and will remain
an isolated system, degenerating into a more disordered state,
experiencing entropy, lying on the floor while drinking West
Sixth IPA, listening to Radiohead, and reading Anne Rice. Or,
she is an isolated system, and will continue to degenerate, splayed
on the floor while drinking Corona, listening to Phosphorescent,
and reading Dorothy Parker. Or, she simply could be crying on
the floor, having drunk six IPAs, and though the song "How
to Disappear Completely" is playing in sympathy, she's not
enthused because it's 1:15AM and she wants to have a reason to
be. Where does Kate Burnham go when she sobs into slumber
and dreams her broken-record dreams about never eating or
drinking but dying in natural disasters, mostly tornadoes?
Obviously, she goes where the chaos is, the random, savage wild.
Let me repeat myself. This individual is an isolated system, an
archetypal island, which will continue to degenerate into chaos,
increasing in entropy, and will continue so toward infinite
uselessness with no exception. She can, however, be acted upon
by a God, or someone who really needs her, who might temporarily
arrest her degeneration by asking her to exist for a reason, woke,
before she disappears completely. Kate Burnham would have
fought against her own predisposition toward decay already, but
it's difficult to lift up from this cold, hard floor, useless actually, if
one believes in Physics and not a God. Kate Burnham believes in
entropy and chaos. Let no one say she *wanted* to believe.

Mother, May I Disappear?

When considering suicide,
    try to think in music, not just
                words,
like an opera is telling this story.
    Try to feel everything at once,
                synesthetically.
Take a bath while listening to
    Radiohead's "How to Disappear
                Completely."
The water swirling down the drain
    is cold, metallic, antiseptically clear,
                smelling faintly
                  of bleach.
Watch, hypnotized, the grey liquid funnel down
    and shiver. Am I here . . . ?
                Is this really happening?
                    Smoke.
The end of the cigarette—crinkled, wispy, bright,
    tangerine orange, glowing beneath
        as you drag slowly—like
           lava
rolling and cooling as it hits salt water. The
    matter-of-fact tapping with extended index
        finger and the falling
                away
of the weak, feathery, burnt tobacco remains—
    a gendered gesture, considered feminine,
        as opposed to flicking the filter with
            one's thumb,
not caring where the ashes might tumble. Share old
    stories to make them new again,
        with younger, older, smarter,
            stranger folks.

The tales told don't change from age to age—
    mouth-to-mouth. "The boredom, and the horror,
        and the glory," to quote
            Donald Justice.
Mostly the boredom and the horror, though.
    Send the ex-lover pictures of empty
        pantry shelves. Remember Grandma's
            permeating aroma
and how, even after she was dead, her house
    still smelled like her for over two years. Beg
        for God to speak. Beg to be
           loved
the way you want to be. The old stories can't be
    renewed. Try to remember what it
        felt like to be connected to your
          mother's womb. Try,
            try again,
and when even that fails, then, you have
    permission to
            disappear.

** Consider listening to "How to Disappear Completely" or "Daydreaming" by Radiohead before or while reading.

Communal Birthday Dinner

with my lover's wife and daughter in early winter season.
Group photo that I take after the celebratory repast:

~husbandwifedaughter~

Group photo that I pose in:

~mistressdaughterwife~

The two leading ladies don't know—or worse, do know—
I'm the festering affair, sitting beside them on the snow-
flocked bench surrounded by blinking blue and green
lights. Wife calls me *adopted daughter*, calls me *Dear*.
We pose for the roles we play:

wifeanddaughterpoised
atthesidesofhusband/father
seatedaskinginSanta'schair
flower-girl-ingpardonsandgifts.
Daughtershoulder-to-shoulderwithmistress
mistressleaningcongenially
towardwife/mother
inthethickofthem
center-stage.

See how all three *shes* wear neck scarves, cross their legs,
fold their hands in passive gesture—hallmarks of our
feminine sense of place and purpose. See the corners of our
mouths turn up, our eye contact with:

~husbandfatherlover~

He catches the moment on his iPhone, purchased on our family plan, supplemented by mistress's income. Photo-bombing from the inner-scape:

themicroscopicembryo
posestoo,fornoone
saveitself,itsfour-week
birthdayarrived,itspicture
stilldevelopingindarkroom
whileitfeedsonthecommunalfeast
ofoursharedbirthdays.

Desire Directs the Footfall

In showing love, you've always been discreet.
My love is flammable, always on exhibit.
You only send me pictures of your feet
    to hang on my walls.

My heart is not a honeycomb. I can't compartmentalize my joy,
adoration, worker bee's devotion, which you don't prohibit.
    But like a Queen,
in showing love, you've always been discreet.

We drones, we love-drunk bugs, can easily destroy
ourselves in our incessant buzz and care, which knows no limit.
    I want to see your angel-wicked wings.
You only send me pictures of your feet.

You're more a fallen god than any angel, or maybe just a boy
whose feet don't point in my direction—from me they aim to quit.
    And like my silent God,
in showing love, you've always been discreet.

I've become a clever bore, exercised every ploy
to tempt you to an indiscretion, where the summit
    of your reluctant care transcends. Why do
you only send me pictures of your feet?

I might belong to you in gesture, a slave feigning employ—
I need your name to make me real—my chains to unknit.
    Spoiled man, pretty little decoy,
in showing love, you've always been discreet.
You only send me pictures of your feet.

Mind Fill

Sometimes, all that is left to thank ex-lovers for are
the puddles of shit they leave in me, the brain attic.
Played like a super-galactic pin-ball machine, higher
points scored for sending Kate's shiniest tokens into
black holes and solar flare traps. Her mental land fill—
a hoarder's she-shed, a WTF merry-go-round of a
non-biodegradable garbage dump.

Daydreaming, she climbs up to grab some *needed* curio,
rediscovering a nightmare instead—about having a
polygamy-themed Thanksgiving dinner with her ex's
wife and child—or she trips over the feeling of his
moustache against her lips or legs when she's fiddling
with a flashlight looking for her misplaced inspiration
or social security number.

Gets distracted cranking away at little jack-in-the-box
shit shows, sucked in by the jingle while she's really
trying to remember exactly what he smelled like—
she blames me for the trouble she has finding the one
thing she's always rummaging around for in this impacted
anal gland I like to call the hippocampus. In this scary
movie, the girl wanders in the attic looking for hope
chests and baby pictures, only to find his terrible recipe
for chocolate chip cookies and a stack of his naked selfies.

I'd like her to stop eating so late, let me defragment myself
without regurgitating the sound of his laughter, triggering
night terrors that rip holes in my coding process, freezing
on a still frame of the unnamable.

Sell Me Something Else

Electric, visually dynamic billboard at the edge
of my town, bought and paid for by a local jeweler,
displays a pair of four-carat diamond cluster earrings,
and the caption reads: *Wife Insurance.*

Should someone graffiti over it, paint a realistic mural
of a giant cock with furry peach sac, glans dripping
liquid gold? The girth and length filling the billboard,
satisfying empty space, and the caption could read:
God Is Not Dead.

That billboard would be as equally offensive, sexually
divisive and painful to look at. This billboard makes me
want to beat in the faces of those who created it. It's a
commandment on display bidding me to do violence,
to hate myself and my own species. How many diamonds
does it take to turn out the lights in the human brain?

Are we magpies?   Philosophers?
Can we eat rocks?   Solid ore?

Every time I pass that billboard I need to know what life is like
for any animal other than a human. I want to die naked and afraid
and come back as something that lives at the bottom of the sea,
where flashy lights advertise death as *death*—if you follow the
bright, shiny things, you're going to get eaten.

Apples to Apples

I tempt my lover with apple pie
still warm from the oven,
filled with cinnamon, pectin,
orange juice, and lemon zest—
vanilla in the vinegar crust.

Rolling the dough, laminating
softened bricks of butter in
its folds, laboring in sensuality.
I know the pastry is ready to be
filled with fruit when it reaches
the consistency of baby flesh.

Basting the top crust with thick milk
and egg, I know that the confection,
impregnated with six Honeycrisps,
will melt in the mouth of him,
but it won't win his trust or respect.
Apple pie isn't a truth serum.

At best, a conversation piece,
a sweetening of the deal,
an ice breaker,
a peace offering,
an apology,
a pleading against indifference.

Tasting so sweet and wholesome,
momentarily filling the gaps
between words with consumption
and pleasure. The fruit I picked wasn't
poisoned. It gleamed, glistened, and bit
back on my tongue when I tasted it raw.

It does not offer knowledge of good,
evil, or anything in between.
It is an apple pie.

A is for apple.
Apples are red. Sometimes.
The scarlet letter was an A.
A is for adultery.
The first sin was eating an apple.
Adultery is a sin.
Apple pie is a euphemism here.
Knowledge is power.
Gaining knowledge was the first sin.
Adulterating apples in pie is prayer.

The punishment of sin?
Debasement in tempting my lover
with apple pie, so that I can warm him
up to me, so that I might enlighten him
on becoming a father.

Lipstick Queen's Perfect Red

—for love of lips.

Rouge Sinner / Red Sinner / Rust Sinner
Any which way I paint my lips, I'm
carrying on the tradition of Hawthorne.
I can't wear my preferred shade and be
a woman without reminders of the tropes
and trifles of Puritan culture.

Cherry / Candy Apple / Currant
My favorite color, the warmest. Burst
my bubble and bash it all to hell every
time I hear a comment about rosy lips,
ruby slippers, ladies of the night wearing
the color of their trade. Slut-shaming culture
mocking the innocence of my infatuation
with the color of my blood oxidized. Drive
me to hate what I find beautiful; make me
pull a Catherine Breillat stunt on camera—
pull taut my labia and paint them the color
of a monkey's ass in heat.

Stigmata / Incarnadine / Sang du Mal
Thank you for teaching me to love my body,
my tastes in looks, clothing, cars, and the color
of my bedroom walls, then scorning me for it
all and calling it woman's sin. I'll paint my lips
the color of nothing, like a mouth agape, and
kiss-print my thoughts on pages in DNA, like
a woman speaking out in the congregation for
the very first time.

**Lipstick Queen cosmetics were branded by Poppy King. She marketed red lipstick as a sinful pleasure.

We're in a dystopia now, Kids.

Almost five months pregnant,
I don't feel the baby move yet.
Vigilante inside me, in spite of
99.9 percent effective pills.

> *Feeling of warmth, radiant,*
> *on my stomach from your hand,*
> *soothing the turbid silence*
> *of the baby.*

I am not a sadist and didn't mean to conceive.
I would never have asked a defenseless
possibility to become an actuality. But I am
a masochist, divested of safe words like *No.*

> *Driving away in my*
> *packed-to-the-roof rental,*
> *leaving you behind in your*
> *denial, waving me off.*

Until I met you.
Until reason, hijacked by hormones, bled out.
Until an ultrasound wand submarining in my vaginal cavity
revealed a heart smaller than a pinhead beating in heat signature.

> *Planned Parenthood waiting room,*
> *smell of Febreze heightening*
> *the panic of coercion to abort. Protesters*
> *picketing for Jesus' running for politics.*

The man I want to die with doesn't want me to have his baby,
so why can't it be thriving in his body, not mine?
The burden of choice placed on the shoulders
of a fifty-six-year-old Peter Pan.

Your daughter's hair smells like yours—
sweet, creamy coffee—child
from your first marriage.
Will his hair smell as sweet?

Son-to-be should feel as real as
your suicide threat, twisting my arm
to invalidate his existence,
naming it less than your own.

Crossing the Kentucky State line,
my own hand radiating warmth on my stomach
in February freeze, dog's head in my lap as I drive.
Extreme nausea affirming my baby is strong, albeit silent.

This is how a new person is brought into being:
caught in middling, born into purgatory,
arriving from the void into a shared experience
that has always been
dystopic.

Craving Control

Eat the cookie—even though I had gone years
without sugar in my diet, you forced the lemon,
blueberry, and white chocolate concoction into
my mouth, parched dry and then flooded with
spit by nausea.

*Top the over-cheesed turkey chili with a sunny
egg*—shovel it down while it's scalding, yolk
melding with tomato paste and cumin like milk
marries with honey.

*The from-scratch gumbo you are simmering
is poison*—innocuous combinations of butter,
the trinity, chicken stock, filé powder, andouille
sausage, and shrimp, all combined to create a
stench unpleasant to heaven.

Make popsicles from pickle juice—*dill* pickles,
with extra white vinegar, the taste of an expectant
mother's low-blood-sugar-induced wet dream.

I do as you say, eat what you want, gain thirty
pounds more than most physicians recommend by
the time my body begins your eviction process.

Fourteen hours of labor alone, my ex-lover texting
to remind me to drink Gatorade, my mother's fists
pressing into the small of my back for hours, even
though I didn't want her touch at all as a mother.
I *had* to let her touch me, to keep the back-labor in
check, roaring through every contraction and
refusing the goddamned Gatorade at every
worried midwife's prompting.

You came at the end of my road, with my heart
rate too high to allow a home birth, after we had
mowed through two tanks of oxygen and pounded
the electrolyte sports-piss in pure rage. Somewhere,
outside of the room, I heard the EMS crew talking

about slicing and dicing my taco, and I successfully birthed you on ugly green shag tarped-over with puppy pee pads.

Within twenty minutes, *you* all pinked-up and breathing deep, I ordered my dinner from the café I had my first job at—a meal which you no longer had any say in. You'll never guess what I craved.

** Thank you, Mom, for your tiny munchkin hands turned into fists, and everything else.

Grandma Nete

Sip on you, tish head—you ain't so muckin' fuch.
You'd teach me all the swears before I was eight, or so.

Tell me stories about traveling cross country on the back
of a motorcycle, with nothing belonging to you but the
clothes you wore and a toothbrush, sleeping in barns.

Teach me to brush my teeth first, then have ice cream
before bed. Scratch my back, legs, arms, until my eyes
sink shut and my four-year-old body shivers into sleep.

Show me how to put my hair up in curlers, pin laundry
on the line; wriggle a worm onto a hook, spit watermelon
seeds out fast and far.

Sing "You Are My Sunshine" to me, every time I wept
for my mother. Promise me a gold star for every plate
I cleaned, every toy I put away.

Teach me I'm not better than other people. Teach me your
favorite fart joke. Let me smell your smell of Aqua Net,
talcum, and Design by Paul Sebastian.

You were my first apple pie, my Mexican wedding cake cookie,
my marshmallow creme fudge with walnuts, and when you
passed away, my sweet tooth ached only for you.

Things My Father's Father Loved

were simple. Easy. Roy Rogers, Gabby Hayes, black coffee, boilermakers. He took to junk guitars, broken radios, leather, lacquer, and cane poles. Smacked lips for custard pie, PayDay candy bars, catfish, green onion dipped in salt, fried anything, and lemon on everything.

Laughed at clean jokes, dirty-bird humor. Took naps on the floor with grandchildren, could soothe any baby to sleep. A tall, thin, wander-lusting local gent, nothing made him happier than good food and long drives to anywhere, neither of which he ever got enough of.

He deserved flowers every day, special dinners, angel food cake every night. Deserved legs un-crippled by polio, to have never heard the word *cripple* applied to him, a man who could walk on his hands better than most can walk on their two perfect feet. Deserved better than diabetic diet plans of the early nineties—dog food.

We forgot about him, dying alone in the nursing home in Puryear, Tennessee. His only living son forgot about his father's happy thoughts, the things that allowed him to fly. Forgot about the tenderness a man raised in the thirties showed to his children, as much as a mother, gently wiping the baby's ass and nursing through fevers in Indiana winter.

I forgot about you, Grandpa, but I wish that you are in a Neverland now, or at least experiencing the imagined peace of non-existence. I've forgotten when you died, only celebrating your birthday every July third, the fireworks announcing your nativity more than commemorating my American liberties. But I still love you and the things that you cherished. I still feel your pulse in the lake, in black coffee, in my changing world. I've learned that what I forget might have loved me, too. A sin I'm learning not to repeat.

Sleeping It Off

Wiping snot and tears
from my face with
a corner of my infant
son's onesie—the reverse
of a mother offering the
sleeve of her blouse, a
makeshift handkerchief.
Singing:

suckle, suckle
cuddle, cuddle
nap, nap
sleepy sleep . . .

Napping with newborn
to escape depression—
the non-postpartum variety.
When he goes down,
I go down, singing:

suckle, suckle
cuddle, cuddle
nap, nap
sleepy sleep . . .

Can't conjure the happiness
my body needs to lift through
exhaustion as heavy as deceit.
Weight of loving an absent
father is crushing confessions
out of me that I don't even mean.
Keep singing:

suckle, suckle
cuddle, cuddle
nap, nap
sleepy sleep . . .

I whisper-sing this song to him—
needing to be held the way I hold
my son, like a mother or God
holds what is most precious and
doomed to live.

Voting Demographics in 2020 A.D.

Make America great again. Donald Trump
campaigning like Julius Caesar to make the
Roman Empire great again, eagle banner
waving overhead a talisman of extinction.
Buy my red bill cap and I'll crown you with
the bays, my dear voters—democracy, putting
a new roof on a crumbling foundation.
Jared Diamond would have choice words for you,
POTUS, about flirting with falling, but words are
just that. No one trusts their sources anymore,
because all the writing on the walls is fake and filled
with lead, like the water in Flint, Michigan, like
the thickened blood of its children, retarding growth
and scrambling the cerebral cortex and hippocampus.

Debase the currency until it dawns on all
that gold is not what we should have been
hoarding—for when the stock market crashes,
when the government collapses from within—
but rather seeds and mason jars full of pickles.
Forget Non-GMO-Verified USDA Organic white
privilege. Should we have been digging holes
in the desert, like Stanley Yelnats, to hide out in
with caches of Sploosh and tequila, waiting for
Jesus to return from the East?

There are curses older than man that we
have been tasked to break, but we have lost
our language, our deep grammar and mother
tongue with which to speak the right invocation—
some words are not translatable from one language
to another, and if they were, they would only
alter the consciousness of the learner, causing
a psychotic break. And then where would we

be? In *a field of black telephones ringing,*
with Emily Pettit, Sartre, and Wittgenstein,
assessing *a problem*?

We were all indigenous once—once we were all
Pocahontas or Geronimo, colonized and penetrated
and left with our language amputated, removed
like an organ harvested from our bodies and sold
on the black market, the dark web. Now we are
sitting on our brittle bridges in middle America,
in the middle of our eroding Highway 66, with a
Ouija board, trying to contact the spirit world
because we don't remember how to pronounce
God's true name. We are asking if we are not alone,
if someone is with us, inviting the demonic. We are
asking to become possessed.

** "a field of black telephones ringing. . . a problem" quoted from "Red Wings Collapsing" by Emily Pettit.

Rehab

I close my eyes and masturbate,
and for the first time
I don't think of you.

I imagine ramming my fist against
thick, sturdy, corrugated
masonry—
against a wall I can't see over
and have to punch through.
I imagine smashing my own reflection,
feeling shards of the mirror shred
through unyielding flesh.

Stroking up and down the walls
of my vagina, massaging my clit,
I don't imagine sex at all.

I whack off while thinking
about breaking bones in my body,
breaking down the bones of houses
and watching them fall. Demolition.
I imagine being drawn and quartered,
flesh fileted from muscle,
all the while screaming to full satisfaction,
until I'm choking on my own blood.

I'm doing the hard work.
My vagina needs rehab after a five-year
and nine-month addiction—situationship.

Didn't you watch your daughter being born?
No, I would never have had sex again,
you protest.

Can't see the beauty in horror.
Couldn't look at the exploding taco
and still want to eat it.
Couldn't peer into the old lady purse
that is my vagina and see all the possibilities,
or go hand diving for loose candies
in the many pockets—
free sweets to filch.

> The gynecologist told me to exercise this
> goddamned vagina, so that it doesn't spit out
> my uterus or bladder like old gum or chew.

Orgasms and massage, apparently,
help muscle strength return after
pushing a planet through that
supermassive black hole—
something that starts out so small
a crochet hook could barely pass through, but
ends up stretching wide enough to allow
even God safe passage.

> She gave me dilators for my cunt to bite down on,
> yoni eggs to hold in my pussy like Eliza held marbles
> in mouth while reciting for Professor Higgins.

Kim Anami wants me to be a well-fucked woman—
lift surf boards, full grocery bags, and bowling balls
with my bionic vagina. She wants it
to chew steel and break boards
with the power of its orgasms.
There is a lot of
vagina-with-teeth imagery
going on in my life.

After giving birth to our son,
I feel like everyone
has been telling me

that my championship belt-winning pussy
has had all its teeth knocked out
and needs dentures. A toothless tiger.

I have spent so much time
thinking about you in every circumstance,
masturbation being no exception.
I don't want to waste another good orgasm
that way. I want to cum so hard
I taste blood in my mouth,
screaming victory. I want my orgasms
to make the walls of Jericho come tumbling down.

I want my bruised snatch
to repair, and for its abject beauty and force
to make you shiver and all your sphincters clench.

Be afraid to face the abyss
of dark matter between my legs.
She's a mean, nasty bitch, seen the siege,
lived through it, and built her next house to withstand
World War III. She spits nails, and she
has an eighteen-month sobriety token to prove
I don't need to think of anything,
let alone you, to let myself heal.

Foster the Children

as a child relinquished / at birth / true love waits
behind every corner patiently / not selfishly
not envious / not boastful / certainly not
proud / it waits / and isn't / easily angered
keeps no records / of unnumbered / unnamed
wrongs it never delighted in / the evils done to it

is waiting / for a truth to match its own / all it wants
is protection / trust / hope / perseverance
to match all such that it has been / quietly tending
in its garden of lonely / love never fails / though
everything / passes it by and away

in donated jackets / mismatched Nike sneaks / true love waits
with a trash bag / hefted over its shoulder / containing all
its earthly moss / that wouldn't otherwise stick / wondering if
the next corner it turns / will be a house that denies / its very
existence / parades it around as trophy / of good works done
children none / feel reason to cherish / un-sustained / but waiting
while the search for donors / surrogates / unique-looking infants
with foreign appeal / continues / or no search happens at all
true love waits for you to fall

Happy Birthday Boy

the waiters sing a song
to my son wearing
his tiny sombrero—
not "Happy Birthday"

something about
all the beautiful girls
flock to him
he's one year old

his beautiful father
has not flocked in
from Florida to sing—
he's hiding

under his wife's skirt
a baby chick chirping
bullshit about the sky
falling if she only knew

he'd been cocking around
How long have you
known Bob? wife-mother
clucks a tongue

hen-pecked paterfamilias
doesn't know
his/my son, Bob,
at all

birthday boy smiles
refried beans spilling
from the corners of his mouth
joyous and carefree at being sung to

by anyone, and who needs a Dad
when you have a song to sing?

muchachas bonitas
vos aqui
el rompe los corazones

Melville Teaches My Son to Be a Man At Sea

—The Single Mother's Bedtime Anthology.

A squeeze of the hand
so dearly purchased
so soon filled with the sperm
when the proper time arrived
carefully manipulated—
a large Constantine's bath of it

A sweet and unctuous duty!
in old times ... this sperm ...
a favorite cosmetic. Such
a clearer ... sweetener ...
softener... delicious mollifier!
my fingers felt like eels,

and began, as it were,
to serpentine and spiralize
under a blue tranquil sky
those soft, gentle globules
of infiltrated tissues—
richly broke to my fingers,

discharged their opulence,
like fully ripe grapes their wine;
that uncontaminated aroma,
as in a musky meadow ...
credit the old Paracelsan
superstition that sperm

is of rare virtue in allaying
the heat of anger—I felt
divinely free from all ill will ...
petulance ... malice ... Squeeze!

squeeze! squeeze! all morning
long … till I myself almost melted

unwittingly squeezing my
co-laborers' hands in it—such
an abounding, affectionate,
friendly, loving feeling did beget
looking up into their eyes
sentimentally … let us all

squeeze ourselves into each other;
why cherish social acerbities?
—Oh! let us squeeze ourselves
universally into the very milk
and sperm of kindness. Would that I
could keep squeezing for ever!

I am ready to squeeze eternally.
Come; let us squeeze all around …
in the wife, the heart, the bed, the table,
the saddle, the fireside, the country …
I saw long rows of angels in paradise,
each with his hands in a jar of sperm …

** Sourced from Chapter 94 of *Moby Dick*, "A Squeeze of the Hand."

How Not to Break Even As a Single Mother

Acquire job at daycare, making $8.30 per hour.

Work forty hours per week, losing over two hours each week to mandatory unpaid lunch breaks.

Don't eat lunch, if you can help it, because skipping meals saves about $6.00 per day.

Around $100-200 is withheld from wages for social security, state, federal, and city taxes.

Get late payment and NSF fees when your boss screws up on payroll, shorts you a week of pay, and asks you to wait until next payday for remuneration.

Lose a week of pay when your son gets baby rabies from daycare and no one else can watch him.

Fall ill yourself a total of four times in your first six weeks of employment, acclimating to cooties.

Pay $55 per week—the discounted rate—for daycare for your own child.

Pay $100-$140 per month in gas for your thirty-minute, one way commute.

Pay $105 per month for your status symbol iPhone.

Pay $150 per month for your car and life insurance policies.

Pay $250 per month for your godsend of an apartment in college country, utilities included.

Pay a total of $110 per month in minimum payments on your three maxed credit cards.

Pay $50 a month for Trifexis—medicine which keeps your two dogs heartworm free in Kentucky.

Pay $36 a month for dog food.

Realize you have no damned business having two dogs.

Pay $4 a month for Medicaid.

Count up the rest that is left over for food, toiletries, diapers, wipes, toilet paper, soap, baby shoes.

Eat lots of hot dogs and baked potatoes.

Eat the cereal your son doesn't consume from his WIC allowance —is that cheating?

Hope that your degree will help you make more than $8.30 an hour when you graduate.

Wish you could afford wine—it would medicate the math and doubts into momentary oblivion.

Write a poem about it.

Consider turning the poem into a lesson plan for a home economics class.

Cuddle your child and know it is priceless and costly, more than a luxury and less than a penalty. Not quite even or broken, you sleep.

Budget Rent-a-Car Commercial
Disguised as a Poet's Breakup Text

—After Matthew Olzmann's "Mountain Dew Commercial
   Disguised as a Love Poem"

So here's what I've discovered, the reasons why our
affair is beautiful and doomed: because you can inflict
physical pain on yourself without flinching and fight
like you live to bleed, but words & emotions leave you
crumpled and sobbing. Because you can shimmy from
head to toe and drink me under the table on IPA night.
Because you have rhythm, can grow vegetables with
green thumbs. Because you memorize every special date,
all the students' names, all the people you've ever loved,
and can recite them. Because you smell the best, like liquid
comfort. Because when I helped you move, twice, you didn't
ask me to move with you. Because you like plants more than
you like people. Because plants can perceive colors that
humans can't. Because I'm always the one taking planes,
trains, and automobiles to see you, and you've never taken
me anywhere. Because you make all your comments and
corrections in green ink instead of red, because green is a
soothing color. Because my name is not among those on the
memorized list of all the people you've ever loved. Because
you have never baked me your famous cherry pie. Because
you have never read any of my poems or articles—not even
the one I wrote about you and your favorite Emerson quote.
Your favorite because he mentions making the world better
by leaving a garden patch (but not a child) as a legacy.
Because when you are happy and joyful, your feet tap and
jitter in disjointed rhythm. And because one day two springs
ago, when you were so relieved that I had the abortion, when
you promised we would be together—even as I was leaving—
there was not enough air in my Chrysler Town & Country
Budget rental, or anything more miraculous than my
getaway drive to Washington, where I had our son.

English Campaign for the Sciences

Kate, the English major, will go far, fast, further.
She will become the first-ever human spontaneous
combustionist to freeze over, go dark. She will be
Miss American Eyebrow Picker of the century. With
her prize money, she will buy ten greenhouses in which
to grow carcinogenic, latex-producing dogbanes,
harvesting the sap for nefarious purposes. She will
use her political influence as a reproductively viable
vesicle to get the first-ever Venus flytrap into office—
will tour the country giving screenings of *The Secret
Life of Plants* for the campaign. She will give readings
at universities of her poems written in ethno-botan-ese.
When the students hear the words spoken, orchids will
sprout through their eyes, staghorn ferns will be vomited
out through their noses and throats, bryopsida funaria
shall bloom across skin like tattoos, and the anus and
genitalia will erupt with male and female apple saplings.
In future, all written language will be replaced with the
written chemical line structure bond formulas of oxygen,
carbon, hydrogen, nitrogen, sulfur, magnesium, sodium,
potassium, calcium, chlorine, and phosphorus.
OCHNSMgNaKCaClP. Separate dialects might choose
to incorporate lesser elements into their lexicon. This is how
new political factions will begin. Kate's final poem will be
printed on a biodegradable campaign button,
coming back as a flower.

Things that Come in Threes

I love you / I am sorry / I believe you
words everyone has access to and no
license for. Mom, Dad, ex-best friends,
your mouths became matches, unregistered
automatic weapons, incendiary.

Each three-worded pot shot hit its mark,
left me full of holes. Three is an unlucky
number, making for choppy sentence
structures and shoddy heartfelt remarks,
especially. Spell-binding phrases become
sacrilegious on the wrong tongue, like
strychnine-laced acid incantations, when we
aren't trained in how to use them properly.

You didn't *believe* me. You aren't *sorry*—
rarely is anyone ever. Your *love* is conditional.
Please rescind your libel as rectification, like
a ruby-throated bird in merciful reverse flight, far
away from that thick glass and damage unseen.

Post Thunderstorm Chi

Driving home late from work Friday night with my son
chatter-boxing and flinging Cheerios in the back seat.
Dark out, slick roads, cloud layer low and heavy makes
the rain on the highway more reflective and the streetlights
brighter. I'm so tired and sequestered in my motherhood
that I think this scene is beautiful.

Before driving home, weeping in the middle of watching
Kung Fu Panda 3 with my sleep-grouchy son—you know,
the part where all the characters have a shared experience
where they learn to harness chi on instinct, because they
love their friend / have to save his life / they realize their
own power is simply being mortal and finite—like a parent.
And they fucking save the panda. Definitely weep-worthy.

No it's not. What is wrong with a woman who gets the feels
in the middle of cartoon drivel, as if listening to Beethoven's
Ninth? Where did my twenties go—weeping over being frustrated
that the God of Abraham is a mute life coach when I was raised to
believe otherwise? Bawling my eyes out over having fallen
in love for the first time, and not being able to escape it.
Make no mistake, I just had a moment with Po the Panda's
noodle-hocking father goose, pushing golden chi through his
flight feathers, like the universe was sending a message on the
Creator's behalf that all this shit is somehow beautiful and
worth it, simply because it's slipping away, like my sanity.

I get choked up over baby videos on Facebook, the ones my
friend sends me of her son playing music on an overturned
pot with chopsticks, singing loud and proud about peeing
on the couch cushions—*I go pee-pees right there!*—
gesticulating to the spot in question with extended chopstick,
like it's a Jackson Pollack. Or the *Mommy, that's poop, that's*
poooop, Mommy video, with tiny little Lincoln Log turd

floating inconspicuously in the bathtub next to the Batman
action figure and beach sand trowel. These shared moments
make the chi rush to my face.

I've turned into something that loves ugly, sad, mortal,
mundane things—the way that streetlights are reflecting
on this saturated blacktop, illuminated by the overcrowding
of university traffic in my tiny town. I cry over the sweet
moments in my son's cartoons, because I cringe over every
moment of ugliness in this life—*mother cooks her baby*
in microwave before calling paramedics, autopsy confirms.

I used to wonder why the hell I was alive, thinking I was
supposed to find my purpose, like some dipshit Princeton from
Avenue Q. Now I think that my accident baby boy was no
accident I need ever admit to—he's the only reason. My mammal
function is fulfilled. I get to spend the rest of my days beaming
chi out every orifice each time he does some tiny miraculous feat,
like keeping the soup on his spoon all the way to his mouth, or
Jackson Pollack-ing the floor. Need I name the paint medium?
I've downshifted my consciousness, become dis-enlightened and
grounded in the grind. I see my son and am still, knowing
the child is God.

Eating Your Way Out

—for the friends we lose to cancer.

I'll cook you the meal
you dream about eating
when you're not afraid
of dying.

I'll make a bone broth
soup—oils from marrow
and tendon clinging to
the sides of the spoon and bowl.

I'll bake a deep tureen filled
with aromatic onion, garlic,
eggs, thick cream, soft cheese,
butter, and pork belly, caramelizing.

I'll have spiced everything
with thyme, cinnamon, white
pepper, cardamom, star anise,
clove—the bitters bring out the sweet.

I'll roast vegetables soaked in
truffle-infused oils, spritzed with fig
balsamic, sprinkled with Himalayan
pink salt, blistering brown skins that crunch.

I'll simmer a savory herbed chocolate sauce
to drizzle over the whole plate—a sauce to
induce visions, lining the stomach with
prophecy, preventing indigestion.

I'll eat the whole table with you,
thinking about Tita's rose petal witchery,
Vianne's spell-bound dinner guests,

and hope that the food I feed kills
the appetite for anything more than
an easy and satiated death. Fold you
into my arms and let you sleep
the sleep of no hunger, the way
you felt in your mother's womb,
before you entered this world
the way you're exiting it—fed.
Full.

My Drunk Kitchen: Kate's New Year's Baby Episode

So there was this one time
    a few years ago, that I was
        cooking your father Tequila Duck
in chipotle orange and adobo sauce.
    I deboned the carcass, shredded
        the meat, spritzed it with lime,
poured the sauce reduction over
    the flesh, and let it marinate. We
        ate it that night on corn tortillas
with tart cranberry relish and cilantro,
    washing it all down with Blue Moon
        and a sense of superiority for being
so creative in the kitchen.

What is my secret to cooking a greasy, old
    water fowl so tender and tasty?
        I marinated myself in as much—
if not more—Jose Cuervo and orange
    juice as I splashed over the duck's
        patted-dry breasts. My mind numbed,
but somehow my tongue survived to know
    how much more spice to add and how
        much sugar to withhold from the relish.
After, I drank straight from the extra-value bottle,
    hitched over my elbow like a jug of moonshine,
        wearing my Santa hat as toque blanche
like a true pagan on New Year's day, still celebrating.

And because your father thought this made
    me appealing enough to sneak with me into
        the laundry room like a closet at a Christmas
party, so you became you, on my stomach full of roasted
    duck and Mexican liquor. At least I am fairly certain that is
        the story of how you were conceived—in love and laundry.

**Title inspired by the YouTube cooking series *My Drunk Kitchen*.

Compartmentalizing on Gratitude

Thank you: for when the power goes out for extended periods,
after storms or power plant malfunctions, for the silence that
follows—the dark.

Thank you: for when the moving company fails to deliver
the contents of our previous dwelling for over a week past the
original ETA, for the stillness, the audiovisual quiet. My empty
furniture-less house feels like a drunk-tank-pink sensory deprivation
experimental Church or temple.

Thank you: for when the internet fails, my phone gets lost, I have
no television, and my car won't run, all on a Sunday, disabling me
completely, legitimately for doing homework, research, scrolling,
steering, gazing unblinkingly at backlighting.

Thank you: for allowing me to do nothing but drink hot chocolate,
take a long, ritualistic shower, nap with my son not once, but twice
in one day, for giving me permission to give no fucks until tomorrow.

Thank you: for paychecks so small that I can't run the race or even
walk it, for the fact that Amazon Prime, Netflix, iPhone upgrades,
cable television, cosmetics, car payments, and name brand, brand
new anythings are no longer options or even tangible temptations,
for robbing me of my empty need.

Thank you: for the disappointments and voracious lack which prove
to me that my conveniences and desires for the unnecessary are
making me sick and miserable, consumerism's pony girl, stuff's
whipped bitch.

Thank you: for waking up remembering that I am not permanent,
everlasting, for when I don't have to do any of these *things* that
make me anything more than just alive, until I'm not.

Absent Minded on the Sunday Shift

Bush's Best Bean Pot Seasoned with Bacon & Brown Sugar—
I am at work, not in my own bubble universe. Beware the sharp
knives, the boiling water, the electrical outlets, and the malfunctioning
meat smokers that zap anyone foolish enough to touch them while
holding anything made of magnetic material. Focus on the breath
in this moment of panic, silent as blood flow. *Be* at work. Fill steam
tables with pans of brisket, pulled pork, queso, chicken, and pre-cooked
macaroni and cheese in a sack. Breathe, mindfully, and feel the poetry
hemorrhage out of every pore, along with all traces of muse. Take
intentional steps; make every movement count. Remember what it
was like to kiss my lover without weeping after. Rub ribs with brown
sugar and French's mustard—smoke for three hours at low temperatures.
Thank the plumes escaping from the smoker for reminding me of my
respiration, to ask it to stop hitching on the words I want to speak to you:
*I would like to stop talking to you for a while. By that, I mean I never want
to speak to you again, but I don't know how to stop. Help me.*

Carpet

unwanted skin of the floor
fake grass, moss, feather lining of the burrow
plasticized, hygienic substitute
hated for never being clean
attracts and holds debris like open pores

dogs preferring grass to do life's dirty business on
but berber stealing a close second to turf
vacuuming for at least 2 percent of your life with a $2,000.00
Dyson—like obsessively popping perennial pimples,
like mowing the lawn, procrastinating,
washing hair that only oils over
the very next day

carpet wear patterns tell the truth—
you only use 8-9 percent of the square footage
of your eight-bedroom, three-and-a-half-bath abode

Bed, Bath, and Beyond is in the kitchen—
throw rugs are to carpet as fallen leaves are to roads—
clutter obstructing travel between
point A and B on cool, clean ground
showing all the stains, like flesh
rip it up, out, leaving the better bones beneath

houses are not nests anymore
hard wood and stone are better support
for angry feet and tired backs
with no rest coming anytime soon
no carpeting, cushioning—
VIP red or otherwise—
just the rug burns

Whoreson

Toddler hand outstretched to grasp a velvet muzzle—the first time touching a real horse, a long-awaited moment. First words were Mama and the neigh noise, so Dada was replaced by the Big Dog. The Cree called them big dogs—*atim*. The Lakota called them sacred dogs—*shunka wakan*. My son just tries to speak horse—high-pitched, nasal vibrato trill. It must have been in his deep grammar from a past life—dogs are OK, but horses are gods.

Squealing with delight as wet tongue descends from between soft, whiskered lips, the popping of the mare's chops, to lick the hand small as a new maple leaf. I don't even have to try to tell him to *keep your hand flat*—the electric excitement of equus radiating through his fingertips, making any movement besides splaying phalanges impossible. The fingers stretch straight, but the toes curl tightly.

Reminded of Michelangelo's *The Creation of Adam*. There is something as uncanny occurring between the boy and the horse. Richard III, begging a horse to escape being a bastard. Wondering if my son will grow up with a father-complex, a chip on his shoulder in lieu of lump, nonetheless marked a whoreson for all the wonder in his eyes in the presence of men and steeds. Where does the instinct to mount the animal and ride come from?

Watching toddler try to hug the long face of the birch-brown mare—flies buzzing and the strong, grassy manure scent not deterring his adoration. My breathing capabilities suspended by emotion, yearning, the ineffable. Why can't we all ask a horse to let us climb onto its back and run away from our languages, ideas, houses, technology—no saddles, just muscles clinging to musculature and speed? Perhaps the first joyride, preceding longboats.

What we are escaping, maybe, doesn't matter—maybe it's the fact that we are escaping on something with a pulse, that is willing to carry and run away with us. Only Pegasus could make the feeling more enlightened. My kid already squirming out of my arms to attempt gaining purchase on the back of the gentle mare as I guide his hungry hand along her neck, shoulder, back, flanks. His god shivers under his touch, and he says *I love you* in the universal body language—laying his head against the side of her, I imagine he is hearing the heartbeat and grooving to its rhythm.

Reasonable Fear

What if I told you
that there was someone
standing right behind you,
that you are not alone in
your house at night, that
there is always an observer
observing you while you
shower in the morning,
standing in front of your
not-opaque shower curtain,
able to see through the plastic
barrier, as though they don't
have eyes to see with, anyway,
but only mouths? Disembodied
hands snaking beneath doors
while you shower or shave,
unaware of the visitor.

What if I told you,
you were right to feel
a moment of panic every
time you had to keep your
eyes closed to the soap
streaming over your face
as you washed your hair,
feeling the kinetic energy
of something, someone,
standing there, about
half your modest height,
champing, gnashing
its teeth, and invisible
once your eyes blink
open through suds, but
nonetheless there?

What if I told you,
that's prey instinct making
you slap the soap off of your
face, every once in a while,
to ascertain whether you're
really alone, safe in your
bleached-white, fully-tiled
apartment bathroom, and not
you being overly imaginative,
weird, or brainwashed by
the horror film industry—
you feel fight-or-flight
instinct coursing through
your veins every time you
close your eyes to get clean
because you are in the presence
of the only apex predator left
for humans to face?

When we turn out the lights,
close our eyes, get quiet—
the sound of breathing, blood
whooshing through carotid
arteries, ourselves, and
something else, pulling
the blankets off of our bodies,
the pillows out from under
our exhausted heads, at 3:00AM,
footsteps rapping through the
house where no footsteps should
be—*Wake up, Mommy, wake up,*
the toddler moans, entering your
bed uninvited. You are
never alone.

Somewhere at the Other End of the Universe

Dear reader,
who are you, and
what do you mean?
What is your favorite
color and your deepest,
most abject fear? I ask
because I really want to
know another human being,
as deeply as I know myself,
before I die. I am afraid
I will never get to.

If home is where the heart is, my heart has
taken cues from Mel Gibson's execution in
Braveheart. Chopped-up and pulled-apart
pieces of it have been stolen, abandoned,
hidden all over the United States, and even
gotten lost in the afterlife, if there is one,
with the people who were the only true loves
I've ever had. My family is shrunken down to
two members, and I feel the smallness of the
world and our lives. Pieces of my home are
tucked away into the cracks in the floorboards
and walls of craftsman houses, buried in gardens,
sunken into sand dunes, folded under a hand
now buried in a casket in New Concord, Kentucky,
and written on the feet of someone swimming
off the Florida coast to whom I no longer speak
but still have sweet nightmares about.

Every time I move, gypsy-like, to follow a piece
of my heart, I'm leaving another piece, another
home, behind, so that I am always expatriate in
my own country. I reach a desired destination to

be reminded immediately that I miss wherever I
have left, and so I am restless, always anxious,
ghostly and haunting my own life and the people
in it with unfinished business. My home scattered
like bones, demolished to make way for superhighways
to nowhere. I make jokes about this situation I
am in. I imagine myself a character in a Douglas
Adams novel—not very *froody*, always forgetting
my goddamned towel, empathizing with depressed
robots, yenning for a planet that is both expendable
and precious because it is too tiny for words. Carl Sagan,
help me out here with your *Pale Blue Dot* wisdom.
I think Arthur Dent might be my spirit animal.

Dear reader,
would you pick me up
as a hitchhiker, and tell me
what you mean by being you?
I'm trying to get home—it's about
1000 miles away from here in
every direction, and I just want
to read your secret thoughts
while getting there.

Coffee Cup

Filled to the brim with Maxwell House, mollified with half & half, sugar,
and spiced with bitters, which he kept for me in the liquor cabinet above
the sink. His breath smelled like Arabic spice after breakfast. His
granddaughter would watch him drink from me every morning,
while she ate her cornflakes or cinnamon sugar toast.

Sleepy-eyed as the creamy-colored beverage I carried seeped into
the corners of his thin-lipped mouth, he would grin. Stubble on his face,
click of his straight but ground-down teeth against my semi-porous porcelain.
I liked the way he cupped my curve—mitten-grasped in his left hand, as though
giving a stiff handshake. His thin skin the same burnt sugar color as my brown
blood swilled. I always assumed he was off-white Indian, with his once black,
then pure white hair, high cheekbones, and tawny flesh. He looked like someone
I wanted to marry, if a mug did such things. I was his constant table companion,
rivaled only by the marmalade.

When his wife would disappear with her crossword puzzle, after the breakfast table
had been cleared, he'd beckon the granddaughter over to sit on his knee while he
peeled the daily orange or banana. Every day she spent with us, she got the first
bite of his fruit and the last sip of our coffee, even though Grandma scolded
about stunting her growth. It tickled and soothed my glazed cheeks, the
licking of her tiny, red tongue to catch my warm tears. He let her drink
my stature-reducing dregs down, including her in our morning ritual,
teaching her our ways. I became hers then, by this rite of coffee—
blood magick of decoctions of caffeine and cream. I am chalice.

These days, she drinks from me alone at her own dinner table,
eating nothing until getting through our second tank-full of chai
tea, which reminds me of his bitters. My porcelain finish is crackled
and stained with age, but I yet bear everyday use. I still have his initial
tattooed in battle-woad blue on my front, *Mr. B.* I hope to outlive the other
mugs, at least until her son—his namesake—turns four, when I dream she'll
start eating bananas and oranges for breakfast again, and letting him drink from
Grandpa's cup, from me, in honor of us, and of little, red tongues that sip warm,
brown tears, missing grandpas, *good to the last drop.*

Letter to My Lover about Their Pets

Your gerbils have taken the wheel again,
my love.
They've come spilling out from between
your issues of *Sports Illustrated: Body Issue*,
from the folds of old letters to your wife, from
the heater vent above your headboard, up from
below the floorboards, and underneath your bed.
Those fucking gerbils are leaking from your
Facebook Messenger, Google Hangouts, iMessage,
and WeChat—who knew you had gerbils in China.

There's one in your trousers,
my dear.
It's escaping through your fly, desert rat in search
of a new burrow to snug itself into, niches to niche.
And it's breeding, lover, breeding the way rabbits
and rodents do, and weaving a tangled, incestuous
web of a family tree. Not even ancestry can account
for all these second cousins, and don't you think
these progeny are begging for animal testing?
Your closets are full of nests—piles of old pubic
hair and shredded Kleenex—pillows for these
goddamned gerbils.

Your gerbils have hacked your hard drive,
sweetheart.
I fear it's a bit late to be thinking of stronger
containment devices, cages, or bigger wheels to spin.
These gerbils are feral. Even the cats won't touch them.
They've CCed your entire contact list and attached their
zip file manifesto. They're liberating themselves, going
transparent, and inviting audits and investigations. Soon,
you can expect press conferences in your living room with
your whole family present, pens poised over notepads.

These shit-mongering gerbils are pulling a Guy Fawkes coup on you, yes, and your mask is slipping, falling into their tiny, furry paws, your crocodile tears. Your gerbils— they got loose, and now, how will you catch your spinning wheel as you crash-land this gun show?

Tough Love, or Why I Sometimes Sympathize with Dolores Umbridge When I Think of You

Breathing all over turning twenty-five,
we fell in illegitimate love, and I commemorated
my quarter of a century giving you the first of many
stolen yet precious kisses, ass-grabs, and you-remember-the-rests
behind a literal bush, in a dark corner of an empty park
parking lot. You were following your feet.

Li^f_ve/Believe, your insteps suggest in ink.

I have a sum total of twenty-seven photos of your
tattooed tootsies to remind me of the life we aren't living
together, and I can't help missing you, wondering where
those feet are leading you so suddenly that you can't even
stop to answer your messages, your phone, your email, or
your legally-wedded wife's inquiries as to why I don't
talk to her anymore and *how long have you known* that I
had *a little boy who looks oddly like you.* Just following a path.

Li^f_ve/Believe, your insteps suggest in ink.

Breathing all over turning fifty-seven,
you've lived longer than your father, and I hope you will
commemorate this with another tat—a tradition of yours.
Not my initials, or our son's, or something cheap like that, because I love you.
Put your feet in the ocean this year with a new life lesson inscribed
in every step you take further away from me—*I must not tell lies.*

Li^f_ve/Believe, your insteps suggest in ink.

Hit Send

Post accidentally sending a text message to his wife
that was meant for my eyes only, he texts me:
I just fucked up.
Ten minutes later, wife is reading—*she asked me*
to make a wish as I blew out my candle, as she held
the phone for me as we FaceTimed our daughter, and
I didn't hesitate to say in my mind "to meet my son."
I'm no longer the patient lady-in-waiting.
I'm a malfunctioning buzz saw.

Can't call it wish fulfillment—he an unpracticed
bulimic, truth splashing out like drunk vomit.
I thank him for sharing her suggestions of going
to counseling and sex therapy sessions by laughing
my teeth loose. He says she's been *sexting* him,
now that his bank account is slinking out the back
barn door along with those wild horses that couldn't
drag her away. I get *Wild Horses* stuck in my head
trying to suffocate thoughts of my post facto family.

I only succeed in iMessaging demands, humming the chorus:
The rice cooker you gave me—I want it back. He knows,
the one I left sitting in the middle of his wife's unmade
bed when she complained he gifted it without asking.
I had nightmares about cooking the rice they saved
from their wedding in its six-cup-capacity depths, eating it.
I want my Kitchen-Aid mixer back. The one I gave his
daughter because it was too heavy to toss on top of the
mountain of belongings I had Jenga-stacked into my rental
minivan to move 2,400 miles across country, so that I could
have her half-brother alone.

Tell your wife everything you ever told me about yourself.
Go to sex therapy and thumb your way through it. I want to

know what Freud would have reckoned about smartphones.
I want you to stop texting me. I never want another picture
of your feet giving me advice that you, yourself, never follow.

I think the new stage direction for this morality play,
instead of *Exeunt*, should be *Hit Send*. He might thank
me later—that I only asked so little of him, while alimony
is rolling out, direct-deposited into her account, funding a
thirty-eight-word mistake he texted three days after his
fifty-seventh birthday, meant for my eyes only.

Mommy Is Out of Order

My customer at table twelve, sitting with her six-month-old son and six-month-old-esque husband, needs a sign to hang on her face while she pounds the Vegas Bomb I just dropped with their appetizer of Don Julio and Crown. A sign posted to everyone, stating that no matter in which combination you press any or all of the available buttons, nothing will come out of her drop-down dispenser.

D7—you cannot *taste the rainbow*. E5—no *breaks* will be given. B3—this is not a game of bingo. F2—I will not *snap into* your slim jim. C4 sticks because it has dispensed more than its fair share of happy endings to suit-and-tie jerks like Da-Da, home late from the office or fantasy football league meetings.

A sign that reads: Stick your hand, your empty cup, into my service port one more time, and I guarantee a malfunction will occur, and I will piss my stream of scalding hot, instant vanilla cappuccino all over your naked flesh pandering for action, not reaction. The customer service number no longer works. Please read management's posted directive.

Mommy to mommy, vending machine to vending machine—*it's ok.* #Stop-PuttingOut. I call my table twelve an Uber, refusing further service, smiling at the future in a high chair.

Conjuring Cups

—for all the grandma poems.

Before there is time to reconcile death in the body,
so much of the grieving becomes figuring out
what to do with all the tea mugs and coffee cups—
all four cabinets of them. Thirty-six in total, thirty-six
portals to the afterlife. How many legacies left in
microwave-safe glass and flower print house coats
can one person lay claim to? Speak the words:
        "Grandma is dead."
Anita Ellen Burnham died. If I weep and whisper
her name into each cup as I sip where her lips rested,
waiting for the draught to cool, can I conjure Nete
back to me in the deep, black witch's brew I call
my mother's dark roast? A collection of cups
to enshrine her dancing dasein.

Basic Needs

My college professor landlord makes batteries and light fixtures out of potatoes and mason
jars. He says social media gives people hairy palms, causes blindness, so he abstains.
Duct-tapes or pastes epoxy over the cameras of his laptops and smart phones, and suggests
I do the same. A special section of his library is dedicated to volumes which teach one
how to survive without infrastructure or economy. He predicts that we will become
a bartering class within the next hundred years. I believe him. I want to survive. I have a son.

I grade papers composed by matriculating high school seniors, which are hand-written,
illegible, and grammatically incomprehensible. These young adults would likely not survive.
They don't know that you can make soap by rendering fat, adding lye, water,
and allowing the admixture to cure. They don't know that harsh soaps help wash away
radioactive material. They don't know that Silly Putty was invented by accident, and
ironically shares certain properties with napalm. They don't remember George Carlin
making jokes about this. They remember Tyler Durden pouring vinegar over a lye burn.

If I could just get them to read the Palahniuk book instead of relying on Brad Pitt's portrayal—
that would be a start. Consumerism is feudalism dressed up to go to the ball to dance with
immortality disguised as cosmetic dentistry, freedom posing as designer clothes, cell phones
chiming the twelfth hour when the spell wears off— those twin towers crashing that told us
we could buy back our identity by working just to pay for all the things we want—who said
anything about need? I just made a non-impulse purchase—a Bear Archery hunting bow,
arrows for mid-size game, field dressing knives. *Why*, my practical, responsible mother
asks—she gets credit for ensuring my survival through infancy, but not beyond it.

Because that soccer mom with her Tervis tumbler, Special K snack bar, and quilted Vera
Bradley shoulder bag, will be the first person to kill me for the last can of Campbell's soup
on the Walmart shelf when Rome falls. I will learn to use a longbow, gut and skin a deer,
eat its sweetmeats raw, salted with fresh bile, like I belong on the food chain. Hopefully,
we won't be trudging down some road imagined by Cormac McCarthy, me telling myself
my son is my Law. That if he is not the eleventh commandment, then God gave none before.

Tick on My Dog

3:45 AM:

I wake thinking so clearly about the eventuality of my own death that I feel I am dying at that moment. Still alive ten seconds later, I roll over and run my hands through the short fur of my mutt's neck—Coon Hound and Great Dane, she is the man in my bed keeping me warm. Fingers scratch against a familiar Kentucky lump in my throat— a bloated little bastard plumping itself on the fountain of my John-Wayne-like canine companion. I find this ioxdidae in the afterglow of night terrors, go a little overboard. This ectoparasite—watching it hyper-drive squiggle its legs through follicle branches of hair, fucked-up-spider-mated-with-a-crab-and-Muppet—incites a maniacal S & D.

4:00 AM:

Armed with a cup of alcohol and a desk lamp used as a spotlight. I spend the next hour combing through fur, removing several more of the miniscule reminders of the last breaths I will take on this planet, the last few inches that blood will slug through my veins after my heart spasms and stops, the last few annoying or appealing sounds that my ears will register, brain process. Tick on my dog, you're my act of denial and revolt.

5:00 AM:

Maybe, as I sacrifice your tiny body on the stainless steel of my kitchen sink—matchstick roasting your exoskeleton until you bloat and burst your last blood meal—I will ritualistically stave off death and win a few more heartbeats of life to live, burning our offering, smudging the room with the pleasing scent of sulfur and clean match wood. Death not being equal for us all, I'm equally sad and terrified at making these trades, scratching these itches.

   I'm too awake.

Motivational Bathroom Poster-Note to Self

Kate, you are living your life like your son unravels the sheets off the toilet paper roll—speeding through calendar squares like the double-ply swatches blindly, hypnotized as when focusing on the evenly-spaced lane markers on the interstate at night. Eager only for the end, for some satisfaction once the core is met, all the days heaped in a messy pile on the damp floor, next to the shitter.

Your son lives the Poetry while you wrestle to write it—all of that *do not go gentle* business is Bob's mantra, soothing through growing pains, being told *No*, the weaning and toilet training, right up until his eyes sink shut in the glow of the side-table lamp. You co-sleep in fear. Most of your best insights come to you while sitting on the john.

You wake in the morning already looking forward to a better, fresher tomorrow, every day into the new year—your eyes cast down, fixed on the pavement of life, stepping over the back-breaking cracks squarely onto the poured slabs of each day, until you run out of sidewalk. You plod so gently. Leaving the side-table lamp on for yourself—you're the one most afraid of the dark since his birth.

**Italicized text quoted from "Do not go gentle into that good night" by Dylan Thomas.

Nabokov Teaches My Son about Standing #*MeToo* Close

—The Single Mother's Bedtime Anthology, Book II.

Lo. Lee. Ta.
       Little beauty in a tartan frock,
           On "*bas*,"
               Leaves I shared pulsated and melted on her radiant limb
                   next to my chameleonic cheek.
               Intangible island of entranced time where Lolita
                   plays with her likes—
           Talking—*into* me rather than to me; she poured words into this …
               receptacle with a volubility I had never suspected she had in her.
       Always count on a murderer for a fancy prose style.

               Ladies and gentlemen of the jury, exhibit number one is what
               the seraphs, the misinformed, simple, noble-winged seraphs, envied.

** Generated via a Berstein "acrostic chance" experiment using *Lolita* as the source text.

No-Fault Divorce

Deny the obvious—plug your ears and close your eyes.
Friends chameleon into strangers, enemies kept close-cuffed.
You can deal with the truth, but you can't deal with a lie.

Heft the weight of this exhaustion, a dead-body-heavy sky.
I'm fine smiles, sycophantic laughter not even liquor could slough,
so deny the obvious. Plug your ears and close your eyes.

Mirror practice, adjusted performance quality of your wrinkled face belies.
Everyone knows you've been Punch-ing Judy, pathetic clown routine—*enough*.
You can't deal with the truth, but you can deal with a lie?

Acting like yourself, posing for pleasing, never blinking, pretending to cry.
Your crocodile tears blind you to dying. Your life's work so much stuff. . .
nobody wants. Deny the obvious—pour bleach in your ears and pluck out your eyes.

Always on, sleeping with one eye peeled, try to sell us—maybe we'll buy.
One day, juicy deceits will dry to ash on your tongue; judges will call your bluff.
You can truck with the truth, but you can't dodge with a lie.

Don't die like a white bird in a golden cage, believing you can't fly.
A tangled web shouldn't be a legacy left for children to unravel—grizzled fluff.
Must you deny the obvious—dot your T's and cross your I's?
We can deal with the truth, but we can't deal with a lie.

Chocolate Cake and Red Wine

—After William Carlos Williams

so much depends
upon

a chocolate
cake

and a bottle of red
wine

consumed in one
sitting

in front of a full length
mirror.

> There is even less poetry in me today
> than in *that* poem
> about a red wheelbarrow.

We're Only Here for the Candy, Jesus

Watching the after-sunset Christmas parade
from my small-town court square with my
fourteen-month-old son, I find myself keeping
my eyes peeled for potential shooters while
diabetic women dressed as elves jettison candy
from vintage fire engines into the crowd where
my son and I stand and observe, tiny hand
outstretched to catch a candy-cane-flavored bullet.

I hold my breath when the police pace themselves
around the corner, where the Robert E. Lee statue
remains, carrying the flags of their fathers, the
regalia of their service and faith. This is the Bible
belt I live in—I hear people whispering *Amen* and
praise Jesus all around me as the mobile nativity
scenes roll by, the Pro Life float funded by Shriners,
and the South-Will-Rise-Again motorcycle cavalry—
the same praise and worship spoken aloud to each
passing theater on wheels.

I'm supposed to teach my son about the innocence
and goodness of life, represented by an old, fat, white
man, or a dead, "white," holy man. Sure, sure. More
like I teach him about reading shifts in crowds, reading
all the banned books first, duck-and-covering, and how
to stay the fuck out of trouble around people who are
more interested in the Old Testament God than his dirty,
hippie son, preaching about free love, voluntary poverty,
shaming the family name with his young and naïve ideas
about *good tidings of comfort and joy.*

Toss me and my kid that made-in-Taiwan glow-in-the-
dark Frisbee from Taco John's, dear housewife dressed
like a reindeer, reminding me of Krampus with your

antlers. You'd make the infant savior scream for sure.
Maybe I can use it as a shield when the fire fight starts—
those liberal college brats are trying to sneak in their
float filled with menorahs, Kwanzaa kinaras, the Horned
God of the Wood, and the "Ghosts of White-mas"—
three riders in White Knight get-up, hooded heads in
their laps, as if severed, on horseback. Apocalypse now.
My son smiles as I catch a string of purple Mardi Gras
beads with an attached button which reads: Jesus Loves.

Sleeping It Off II

best friend, lover, ship
gently down the stream
of doubt I *merrily, merrily,*
merrily . . . cast away the
sound of your laughter—
tolling, round, calling
your faithful

row, row, row my boat
through a thunderstorm
of night terrors about
dying with nothing
finished—no lightning
bulbs flashing like
lifetime achievements

row, row, row
my half-deflated
Zoloft dingy down
every little stream,
searching for the only
one that floats my son's
father back to me

that sunflower, fresh cut,
alone in a vase by itself—
the only gift you ever gave—
looks grey in my yellowing
memory *gently, gently*
down the stream

waiting for flower fetish
to trigger worship—irked
heart of a woman who

worships being triggered,
who dreams about a life
she will never have
   ... but a dream

Reasons I Might Be, and Probably Am, Going to Heck

Doesn't believe in Santa Claus, does believe in fairies, and is undecided
    about Jesus.
Owns three IPhones, one IPad, three IPods, two Samsung Galaxies, just
    because—the numerology of modern day slavery.

Weeds and gardens to *beautify* instead of growing food.
Commits mass murder of: ants, spiders, flies, mice, rats, fleas, ticks, wasps, etc.
Eats all the plasticized, processed things/animals because they taste good.
Follows directions on shampoo bottles and showers as if water will not be
    running out in Cape Town on April sixteenth, all taps off.

Makes fun of all religions almost indiscriminately while fantasizing about
    kamikaze fighting God. Doesn't make fun enough of being an Amazon
    addict or binge watching Netflix.
Yells at her dogs like they're inferior beasts. Abusive Species Supremacist.
Won't forgive father for being a racist, homophobic abuser.
Patronizes fast food restaurants and grocery stores that throw out 60 percent
    of what they serve/sell.
Allows her one-year-old to have sips of her coffee.
Buys anything and everything made in China, the outsourced slave-nation
    poster child.
Votes but doesn't live outside her box—where was she at the women's rally
    or the pipeline protest?
Doesn't worry about her own soul, yet tries to prove and nurture its existence
    in others as an escape from her own failures—i.e. slight Messiah complex.

Fails at being both a good human and a good animal—ignores instincts,
    intuition, logic, and inspiration, all.

Never does anything meaningful, like seeing the world beyond a screen,
    breaking bad rules.
Judges people based on whether they talk about the weather.
Talks about the weather with people she doesn't like/respect/have interest in.
Sabotages herself often, simply because failure and self-loathing becomes addictive.
Quotes *that* Gotye song, but doesn't want to pay copyright fees.

Thinks that a good way to make up for any failure or mistake is to cook for people.
Sees no end to this list.
Ends on this number because it's even, when really, nothing else is.
Made you count the lines.

Never Be

afraid to leap, fail, or fall hard, my only son.
You will anyway. Never fear to spit it out—
the truth—but don't forget to swallow pride and
bitterness, regurgitating joy. Don't be shy to wear
your hair down to your ankles or so high and tight
your scalp shines through. Don't dress to impress
anyone except your own skin.

Don't fear to wear as many colors on your face
as you feel thrumming in your chest, see reflected
in the eyes of people who don't love you. Don't
hesitate to love at all, because it's likely life will
leave you parched for its reciprocating quench.

Don't be afraid to lose everything. You will anyway.
Wake up each day afraid not to end it satisfied with
your struggle. If you didn't smile, weep, or scream
in ecstasy or agony, you probably did it wrong. But
no surprise—you'll do it wrong. Screw up in rainbows.

Never be the version of yourself that someone else
paints for you. That's your job, your signature, your
mortal right. I doubt this is your 777th reincarnation,
and so this is your first and only chance to be the
flower, most beautiful just before wilting. Never be
afraid to die—you will anyway, my only son.

Things in Bottles

Edinburgh city center at nine o'clock
at night—walking past Boots Pharmacy
thinking about you, lover. The sun still
up, but the storefront sign is illuminated,
the blue *Boots* insignia glowing like a
chakra, an icon, emblem of youthfulness
promised as advertised. You keep asking
for full frontals. Do I go in?

Buy a parcel of bottled baby
soft skin? If I wear it well, will
someone worthy—you—wonder
at me, " ... to see her was to
love her, love but her, and love
forever?" Boots No. 7 love potion
at 9:00 PM, can you purchase my
romanticized future with a wink
and a wiggle? Please, no.

Please stop advertising the
convenience of Apple Pay and
youthful glow—you'll only sell me
buyer's remorse settled into the
lines of tomorrow's pillow creases
in my cheek. Poison at my fingertips,
every time you ask me to smile, babe—
the "mortal drug" spilling from
between my spread lips, "soon-speeding
gear as will disperse itself through
all the veins that the life-weary taker
may fall ... "

**Quoted text is sourced from Robert Burns and *Romeo & Juliet*.

74

Post Infidelity Support Group Brainstorm

How can you do this   to me?   It's because   I got fat, isn't it?   You're a narcissist   playing on another   codependent.   When are you going to move out   into an apartment?   I don't care   that the house   is in your name, you let me   move down   here with you   like a fool.   I could have   stayed in our old house   and found love...   How often do you talk to her?   Of all the women   you've "been friends with"   in the last 27 years of   our lives   together, which   ones did you bed or   think of bedding?   I don't want you to talk   to your pre-verbal son's   mother,   just your pre-verbal son; you can figure it out.   Why, when you   always told me you liked   my big boobs,   did you cheat with someone   with absolutely no tits at all?   I know I haven't   made any fervent attempts,   amorous or otherwise,   to be romantic or spontaneous   in the last fourteen years, but how about   we break out the lube and give it a go   in between   exit counseling   on our marriage?   Please explain   to me how   you could play   husband and wife   in our house, right under   my nose,   for three years?   How did it   feel to watch   her make me   breakfast   every morning   and wake me up   for work and drive   your daughter   to school—then fuck   her at day's end?   How could you   let her bake our daughter's   milestone 16th birthday cake   and let me invite her   to our anniversary   dinners, which   we shared with others   because we couldn't share   them   between ourselves? Did you enjoy   doing her? How did   you do her? How often?   You know   she got pregnant   on purpose to trap you,   right?   In my naiveté   I hoped   that she left town   so abruptly because,   though I knew   she loved you,   she realized she couldn't   have you.   Little   did I know   she'd already *had*   you. In my naiveté   I hoped   that maybe she   had asked you to just be a sperm donor,   so that   she could at least have your child—   and in your vanity you couldn't   refuse   such a flattering request.   I want   half your retirement,   half your social security.   I want you to   pray with me. I want to   give you   a blow job. I want you   to ask   for my   forgiveness. I want her   to ask me   for my forgiveness. Why are you   still   talking to her?   Can I   sleep in your bed   tonight?   Why aren't you   attracted to me   anymore?   Why can't you   just ask   God for   His forgiveness? I can forgive   you   because He   is my rock.   I don't   believe anything you say   anymore.   She will   dump you   when you are   too old   to get   an erection. You don't   know what   love is.   I don't   want you   in the house. Let's   work   this   out.

Bat in My Bedroom

You remind me that I'm not ready. It's 2:14 AM on the second morning of your visiting, and my hindbrain knows better—jerking my sleeping son by the heels to the edge of the bed and scooping him into my arms to run from the room as you flap overhead, I am my Neanderthal predecessor manhandling my young in the flight from tooth and claw. Danger escaped, my evolution kicks in and my fingers flick to my phone—a quick Google search for the CDC guidelines concerning bats and rabies and sleeping bodies.

I used to be a microbiology major, Batty. I wanted to be a doctor working in a level-4 clearance laboratory, touching Lassa and MRSA, Ebola and Anthrax. I wanted to enact the Milwaukee protocol on third-world rabies patients. But I'm a poet now, and a mom, so fuck that. I want to know whether my son needs immunoglobulin and four shots in the arm of antiviral medication. You fucking bat, I'm not going to sleep for a week looking for you, and my son is sleepy and screaming at me to stop scouring every inch of his flesh, especially what wasn't covered by his long-sleeve footed pajamas. If he could get sunburn from flashlight bulbs, he'd have a tanned hide, because I'm worried I can't see where your tooth or your claw grazed his skin. *Shit.*

I want to catch you, you poor little bastard—trap you in Tupperware, send you to a laboratory where zombified interns will kill you for your brains. Perhaps humans are the bat version of the zombie apocalypse, with our industrialization of all natural habitats and ravage of resources, but I want your cerebral tissue dyed and smeared on a slide anyway, because I'm not ready for my son to die. This time, I'm embracing survival of the fittest, taking advantage of my unfairly won position on the food chain. I want *my* offspring to survive.

If it comes down to my brain or yours, it's going to be my son's noggin that rises to the top of the pecking order. Sorry, not sorry, you vector in flight, inches above my head. In another life, I'll gladly fly and die in your shoes, but today I'm the upright, bipedal, mammalian, pissed-off-at-3:45 AM

Mother armed against microbes in reservoir host. Orange butterfly net in hand and a wet towel to throw over you after I've knocked you senseless to the floor, I'm defending the den. God help the small things, because I'm certainly the monster in their nightmares when they are going bump in the night under my bed.

Age-Appropriate Rating System

Amidst the usual titles— I remember being four and
Sleeping Beauty, The watching Throw Momma
Little Mermaid, The from the Train, Impure
Great Mouse Detective— Thoughts, The Unnamable.
So, a murder/comedy noir, an 80's updated morality play,
and an H.P. Lovecraft adaptation inculcated my mind as much
as any passive aggressive Disney animation could or did.
I think about this about boundaries—
education as what we can and
I teach my can't throw
two-year-old in the toilet.
I think about it as know what I am
I grade eighth grade getting myself into.
English papers for my I have a meme for grading
friend in Cincinnati, eighth grade English:
because I want to Clint Eastwood in
Heartbreak Ridge saying
"Clusterfuck."
Come to think of it, I watched that movie when I was *five*.
Let the children watch they'll be loquacious.
R-rated 80s dramas, Furthermore, they'll
and by God, they know how to cuss,
will learn to speak swear, and curse
their mother tongue— like Anthony Hopkins
was directing them for the stage. This is what I hope for my son.
Dora the Explorer, not to mention the
Paw Patrol be damned, critical thinking skills
because they won't teach he will pick up by default.
my son empathy the way The alternative vying for
that *Amadeus, Dead Poets* my son's attention is
Society, My Beautiful videogame violence
Laundrette will, with no consequences
and consumerist advertising.

So, yes, when I put my son   *The Name of the Rose* while
   down for his nap, and   my son sleeps, and the
      when I have a movie   1997 adaptation of
         day in class with my   *Lolita* while my female
            young and impressionable   students take notes on
               students, you can count   Freudian versus
                  on me to be playing   feminist consent.
         In my classroom, there are no banned books,
                     or films.

Be Both

Sometimes, talking with you feels like
being in the garden of Eden—you, an
Adam and Eve splice, and I, the serpent.

> *Play now the dragon, now the dove;*
> *both parts are useful in affairs of love.*

I try to test your arguments, try to hear
your side, but it's exhausting hocking
knowledge like Vanna White to someone
who preserves their ignorance like youth.

> *Be yours the form that will o'er all prevail,*
> *an angel's features, and an adder's tail.*

Friend, ship, my idol to covet, I worry
that this apple is beginning to rot in hand,
my tongue tied at the fork. Trust in me when
I tell you, you are the god of your path out
of this place, which isn't as perfect as we think—
it's just a garden.

> *What e'er your morals, every look must be*
> *dressed in comely garb of purity.*

I'm tired of filling your blanks, turning
your letters in too-tight sequin gowns,
smiling even though you're stuck on
guessing the wrong consonants and
over-spending on vowels. I took my
poisoned desserts, am leaving this false
utopia, dressed like a whore. Carrying
a child on my hip, reciting the gospel
of every would-be God who strikes my

fancy, not stumbling on my words or
tripping on the stones that hail down on
me, a witch, a wiser woman.

** Quoted text is sourced from William Dunbar's "LXXX The Tretis of the Tua
Mariit Wemen and the Wedo."

Between the Carpet and the Driveway

Nuclear family living in three bedrooms, grooming in two
and a half baths, island kitchen, eating in dining room, greeting
in foyer, entertaining in den, resting in study, parking in two-
car garage, hiding in the basement.

Village and self-sustaining farms lost to single-family tenement,
to shag and avocado green foil brocade dreams of ticky-tacky
housing developments, manicured lawns, sprinklers in drought
season. Men's mansions succumbing to post Cold War indifference.
The down comforters incinerate, plush bathroom mats curdle in
microwave's clutched fist, the new status-symbol Lincoln MKX
evaporating into heavy metal inhalation, at first missile's impact.

House no longer a home, instead an excavation of Pompeiian
tomb. The heart lives elsewhere—before another Prime order
is one-clicked into shipping launch countdown, consider new
chest cavities. Consider roads to nowhere, just outside the front
door. Consider wagon caravans, consider horses, consider running.
Get out.

Popsicles

When your stepmom dies, you become the poet again.
You revert to referring to yourself as *you*, because that
creates a satisfying sense of distance from the self—
from having just watched how the muscles finally ceased
to flex in the jaw and face minutes after actual respiration
ceased, which was actually a couple of minutes after the
pulse had ceased to jump in her jugular because her heart
had already arrested. You talk to your stepbrother like
you are not distancing yourself in ways he has already
done so—*Mom just died; she is at peace now.*

Later, you will become the anger-loafing cynic, liken her
death process to a fish flopped out of water—the silent
gasping motion in her cheeks like gills flapping, teeth
displayed by wilted, drawn-back lips, body dehydrating
in the over-air-conditioned bedroom. Just like a fish—
when the oxygen wasn't getting past her nostrils, though
her eyes were wide, unblinking, her shoulders slightly
shrugging, the jaw working as though she could chew
the air into her; but she was gone, even then. Hospice
offered the morphine that burned her throat, hydrocodone
that made sleep fearful, oxy that made her shake.

On the morning you arrived to be with her, you bought
useless groceries—foods her body might accept when
food was an affront. Kombucha imbued with dandelion
and marshmallow root, licorice, chamomile. Flax seed
oil for the lignans that fight some cancers and accelerate
others. Naked Juice because your father broke the blender.
Bone broth out of a carton because your parents have
been poor for a long time, don't own a stock pot or a
functional crock pot, and because you have to administer
the other opium-derived medicines that make the broth
a nice idea but a moot point. She wants the popsicles, though.

The Outshine, No Sugar Added popsicles—orange ones—
that's what she eats. She consumes one, then two with your
son. The orange ones are his favorite, so they raise their
popsicles to each other. Her tongue stretching out to the stick
in her hand, the act of wrapping her lips around anything a task
she has grown unused to, the atrophy apparent. Your partner
asks if you took pictures of your son with his grandmother
sharing popsicles, and he is disappointed you didn't. She
didn't want pictures documenting it. And that is the last
food she eats—an orange popsicle—like some inmate
ordering their final entrée and being weird about it.

Before she actually died, you bought more, another
whole box. This time the frozen juice bars, but she
didn't wake from the last several doses of oxy, her
eyes sunken and flat. So, the nostalgic neurotic
that you try to be, you raise your popsicle to your son,
proceed to eat the entire box with him, chased with
a pot of coffee and the image of your mother rigid, sallow,
mouth locked open, brown bile slivering down her cheek
onto the gurney, wheeled out the door of your father's
house by the funeral home directors. Her last supper
was cold, sour, sweet, hard to eat—purging everyone
who partook on an empty stomach.

Creaking Toddler Ligaments and Growth in Other Places

Waking to the quaking / shaky wakeup cry of *Mama* / I leave
your side to be by his / fall asleep unintentionally / sneak back
into our room / four hours later to / find you retreated back
to your side of the bed / beyond reach. I wake in the night / still
crying for you / even now / jealous even of the few inches crept
between us / the soft whining pleas for comfort / chewed out
of my weathered nipples. After periods of starvation / over-
consumption and dysphoria are the Rorschach tests / determining
whether our hunger stems from / need or projective desire. Will
we ever feast again? Will we turn our noses away / from the
after-crumbs of / years of imagining the perfect / satiation? I am
a growing girl / feeding a growing boy / hungry for the bread
of your body and breath / not the dough you bring to the table.
My bones ache in any absence / of your savor. Come back to my
side of the bed / sit me to table / spoon feed me / from head to toe.

Comestibles

Scrape the "slate-grey mold" off of
the damned biscuit and eat it
anyway, he mocks me. Carve it off
of the oranges, cheese, cabbage.
Skim it from the surface of the
bean soup, the buttermilk used
to make the biscuits. We tend to
throw out anything with pimples,
except ourselves. I get the word—
comestible—lodged in my head
like a bad song, like the lump
lodged in my throat as I watch
him eat the biscuit, dripping with
butter, noticeable dark specks
still clinging to the crumb. The
word comes from the Latin, which
I learned during lunch hour in my
sophomore year of high school—
comestus/comedere, which means
to *thoroughly consume.* We eat
a lot of the food bound for the
leper colony; haven't been sick
yet. We also swallow down much
more of what we really want to
say, thoroughly chewed-over,
than we chow on decayed edibles.
We have yet to find an antidote for
the blood poisoning that has resulted—
my lover, his family, and I.

Invasive Species

Carrotwood, Rosary Pea, Brazilian Pepper thriving
in my backyard, pitching rashes in the palms of my
toddler when he pulls on the pepper bush's roots,
scattering the lawn with bright berries looking like
miniscule Easter eggs, cinnamon candies—two will
burn the tongue and induce vomiting, the other will
shut down the kidneys, liver, and spleen. Medicine
and poison walking a fine line of dosage.

Some plants were never meant to cross the oceans,
others were guided by the providence of avian gods.
Some of these trees in my backyard were worshipped
before any god asked for offerings of death. Trees that
acted as the first Christs, growing, bearing fruit, giving
it away for the taking—body and blood—healing the
sick, raising the dead, coming back to life in the spring.

For every physical malady, a green answer, but who
looks in their backyards for counseling on their social
order issues, international relations problems, economic
and social failings? Who prays to a pepper plant?
Who listens for the voice of something that can at least
be seen, tasted, touched, smelled? Who is a medium for
communicating with flowers? The species that speak
languages we have never really tried to decipher—those
voices should be tried before anything else, ancient tongues
preceding the evolution of man, the invention of God's
image. What if the carrotwood is trying to warn me like
Douglas Adams' dolphins—*So long, and thanks for all
the Round-up* . . . ? Signed, the birds, the bees, and the trees.

Big Boy Panties

First foot, second foot, slinking past the knees,
silky against thighs and cupid's cheeks—a rite
of passage. The first article of clothing a boy's
father imparts—a pair of cotton-nylon undies,
two sizes too large—the giving of the britches
to signify a male bond. I smile and call them
big boy panties, knowing that I gave the babe
his first skirt—grey plaid, a Scottish wool kilt,
which didn't fit at first either. We dance
bare-assed beneath tartan frocks to Bowie
cooing about power and voodoo, waiting
for underwear tumbling in the dryer to come out,
magically sized to fit. Skirts are better for toilet
training—easier access. I joked with Daddy,
he's already christened them, as I washed away
evidence of the still-pending toilet-trained status.
I gave the child his legs, his bottom, and everything
above and below, I console myself. I am the soil,
Mommy, cotton pants can't erase. Won't I miss
moon-dancing with this changeling child?
A cuter curtsey will never be seen again—
my boy's man-buns peaking from beneath
the pleats—all grown up.

My Lover Gave Me an Alarm

Earlier this spring—no, January winter—I told
you about how, before dawn, I would let the dogs
out into the backyard and suddenly feel like I was
back home in Kentucky, in my grandmother's house
on the lake, because of the birds singing. Orioles,
blue jays, whippoorwills, finches, the occasional
dove. I was re-washing the coffee mugs you had
left in the drying rack, brown rings of stained,
congealed cream you don't know to scrub through—
you're not a coffee or tea person, just a *me* person.

My house on the lake, the one I was strong-armed
into selling to square up my debts, shortly after our
son was born—the earnings meant to provide a nest
egg for baby and me. All I have to show for the *motivated*
sale now—the 2007 Chrysler Town & Country I drove
from Indiana to Florida to reunite with you. It needs
new tires, a tune-up, a full detailing we can't afford here.

Ever since I told you about the birds, though, most days
you wake up before I do and open the front and back doors
to their screens, letting the songs inside, and I wake to the
feeling of being back where I belonged. I listen hard then,
like I do with my ear pressed to your chest at night—
Beethoven deaf and prostrate, ear suction-cupped to the
floor just beneath the grand piano with the sawed-off legs,
weeping for the music he knows is present, able only to feel
the throb echoing in his taut flesh. Everything caught in the
memory of sound—solipsistic—but not the sound itself.

I hear the birds, but they're sojourners here, passing through.
My grandmother is dead, someone I mowed through, a comfort
I ate too quickly and didn't taste, lost the recipe for. Her haunted
house—I let it go. Being here with you, I am haunted only by birds

in winter, your heartbeat twenty-seven years older than mine, receding faster than I can savor. I'm renting a house with you that neither of us will haunt. Too many trades, too many birds, songs escaping with them back to where I no longer belong. I'm prostrate, ear pressed flat, listening too hard for something I can't hear anymore, only feel the throb of—alarm bell of losing it all.

Driveway Moments

Sitting in the sunlight, hot-boxing the cab with infrared heat and watching the ice melt rapidly off of the roof. The coffee makes the moment taste like it feels, but then you have drunk it all and the light has changed.

***

Mirrors for all directions and reflective glass, headlamps, and flickering signals in the night. Everything in view, yet, the blind spots you never recognized. And then the mirror in the visor—checking your reflection in the half light, before starting the ignition, you make sure you're still there.

***

Sometimes you park for hours before going in. The driver's side has a gravity that tows under like the pillows and blankets of your favorite bed. Getting out, it hurts to breathe. On weeknights, you sit and scry through the doubled-paned storm windows like mirrors or mouths expectorating the light inside—and you don't want to imagine that there is a door, just windows and a chimney.

***

On Saturdays and Fridays the parking is immense. You disengage the engine and pocket the key, switch off the headlights. Your head presses and tests the resistance and solidity of the steering wheel or the side window, which are warm and cool. The force of acceleration remains in cell memory. You think; you swallow. When you get up to leave, you finally take your foot off of the brake as the tension recedes.

***

The brick, anonymous stare while you splay out, expand, and occupy every available space of the vehicle, like on a couch or a sofa. Toes pressed against the glass—heat and cold on the feet together. Torso twisted to rest your rear and your chest, head in the back and the legs in the front. Summer with the sunroof spotlighting a supermarket parking lot picnic. Potato chips stuffed into the seat cushions, channel surfing on the radio while reading *The Sun* and *Vogue*.

At 5:30AM, forcing the weak electric lighter to toast one more Winston before the element fails, waiting in line at the drive-thru espresso stand with a full punch card and just-brushed-your-teeth appetite. The engine revs a little. Air in the lines. David Bowie's throb cuts out for a news break inside the coffee shack. Guy Noir zips up for a twin announcement of nuclear attack in your truck while you slip Kelly the tip.

You drag on your cigarette, buts it's already gone out. New papers and no matches. Someone with a UK accent keeps repeating themselves about body count or Geiger count, and you drive halfway to school before pulling into a resting field and leaving the truck where it stays. The gravity is gone, and the moon is still up, low-slung and orange. Walking toward town, the coffee chills and a layer of film congeals over the surface of its volume, and you still don't have any matches. When they said the nation would respond in kind, with force, you remembered pulling out of the front yard for the first time in your first truck, and how good it felt to get away and drive.

Taste of You

The most intimate words I've ever heard spoken to me
apply to more scenarios than sex—*I miss the way you taste.*

Except sex is everything. Stop playing. The first food
we consume—a mixture of ourselves and our mothers—

amniotic fluid, skin cells, lanugo, urine. All we can be
expected to crave thereafter is flesh. Breast is best, feeding

an oral divinity that can't be shamed into total submission.
If you like to swallow, you're not alone. If you see the kink

in communion wafers—the transfiguration—just take it for
the synchronicity it is. Before I met my partner, and before I fed

my son my sweat, blood, colostrum, milk, or bullshit, I missed
the taste of an absent mother. When I fail to savor tears or saliva

or other secretions, I am reminded that I am missing that connection
with a god I no longer have a name for and always miss the taste of.

Notes

Sin Eater

A sin eater is one who consumes and takes on the sins of another by means of a ritual meal, in which bread, salt, and sometimes wine are placed on the body of whomever wishes to be unburdened—a version of Christ's last supper. Not an orthodox practice.

Shadowbox Menagerie

A shadowbox is a framed cabinet-like case, hung on a wall, that houses different curios and small objects. They can be made from old medicine cabinets, or, in this case, from old printing press letter trays.

Definition of Insanity

1841, Essays by Ralph Waldo Emerson, Essay III: Compensation, Page 88, James Munroe and Company, Boston, Massachusetts.

Clausius and Thompson's Second Law of Thermodynamics

This poem owes everything to the genius of Matthew Olzmann's original work, except, perhaps, for my different and possibly danker taste in beer and sources of entertainment.

Dreams of natural disasters, specifically tornadoes, are often indicative of feeling out of control and/or being stuck in a prolonged high-stress situation. Like an affair, or a lifelong existential crisis, or both.

Desire Directs the Footfall

It is said that the direction in which someone's feet, particularly a man's feet, point while talking to/engaging with you is indicative of whether they genuinely like, are attracted to, or are comfortable around you.

Lipstick Queen's Perfect Red

If you haven't seen *Anatomie de l'Enfer*—*The Anatomy of Hell*—directed by Catherine Breillat, you owe it to your mother's hooha and/or to yours.

Voting Demographics in 2020 A.D.

"Red Wings Collapsing" appears in Emily Pettit's collection, *Goat in the Snow*, published by Birds, LLC.

Rehab

Kim Anami just dropped in with a sack of cannon balls. She says she wants to teach us all vaginal kung fu.

Foster the Children

Rob Scheer founded the nonprofit Comfort Cases, donating thousands of backpacks fully-loaded with the essentials of personal care to foster children all over the country, though he is based out of Rockville, Maryland. Having been in the foster system himself, he remembers having to carry all of his personal belongings in trash bags, wearing hand-me-downs from strangers. Married to his partner, they have adopted four children together and have made a point of ameliorating a problem in this country that we are all-too-willing to ignore. Children are being raised by an institution that offers no comfort, no real care, just the necessities, growing up without any real sense of place or family.

Poem references 1 Corinthians 13 in the Bible.

Post Thunderstorm Chi

Avenue Q, this is what you do with a BA in English.

Eating Your Way Out

Reference to Tita and Vianne from the films *Like Water for Chocolate* (1992) and *Chocolat* (2000).

Reasonable Fear

The fear of children is called pedophobia. I find this unfair.

Letter to My Lover about Their Pets

WeChat is a Chinese smartphone app much like Google Hangouts and Facebook Messenger. It allows users to translate messages to and from Chinese and transfer money via the app.

Conjuring Cups

Dasein, in existentialism, is/encompasses human existence, pure Being.

Reasons I Might Be, and Probably Am, Going to Heck

South Africa issued a warning to the inhabitants of its largest city, Cape Town, that they were fast-approaching a "day zero" on which water reservoirs would be too low for plumbing to work in the city. The reaction to this announcement actually turned the consumption around and prevented the water run-out from actually happening, at least thus far.

Bat in My Bedroom

Since the Milwaukee Protocol was first enacted as a trial and error treatment of a confirmed case of rabies, it has failed in every subsequent trial on humans. Rabies is still 100 percent incurable (except in the case of Jeanna Giese) in all patients who have developed symptoms. Thus, the CDC recommends that anyone who has come into contact (a bite, open wounds, mucus membrane exposure) with a bat, or where the bat was found in a room with sleeping persons and could not be caught for testing, be vaccinated on the chance that they could have been infected without recognizing that they were bitten. The shots are very expensive and not covered by Medicaid or many other insurance providers. There are some cost-relief programs partnering with the companies that produce the prevention vaccine, however. It is much more cost effective to receive the vaccine administered where no infection has occurred, as in the case of certain pest control workers and forest service personnel.

Driveway Moments

For the record, nuclear war would likely never be announced in the media, for the simple purpose of avoiding mass panic in the little time left for dispensable citizens to experience life before imminent death. Cheers to that.

Acknowledgements

Thanks and appreciation to *Literary Orphans* for publishing "English Campaign for the Sciences," to *Poets Reading the News* for publishing "Voting Demographics in 2020 A.D.," and to *Triggerfish Critical Review* for publishing "Be Both."

Special thanks to Birds, LLC, for giving me permission to quote Emily Pettit's poem, gratis. Copyright law is impossible if you're a poet. Y'all remember to cover that topic in your MFA programs.

www.ingramcontent.com/pod-product-compliance
Lightning Source LLC
LaVergne TN
LVHW021551080426
835510LV00019B/2473